A Woman's LOVER

By Yvonne Hampden

Copyright © January 2005, 2009 by Yvonne Hampden. All rights reserved. No part of this book or the related files may be used or reproduced in any form or by any electronic or mechanical means, including storage and retrieval systems, without the prior written permission from the author, except by a reviewer who may quote brief passages in a review.

For Information address:
A Ymah Rivera Publications
Yvonne Hampden
PO Box 304, Yonkers, NY 10703
yhampden@yahoo.com
yvonnehampden.com

Library of Congress Cataloging-in-Publication Data
Hampden, Yvonne.
A Woman's Lover/Yvonne Hampden. First edition.

ISBN: 0-9744086-1-1

Text design by Angela Batchelor/Batch-O-Grafix
Edited by Dan Rustin
Printed in the United States of America.

A Woman's Lover

By Yvonne Hampden

Other books by Yvonne Hampden

The Reacquaintance of Love

Acknowledgements

I would like to take this time to thank my family members who have been involved in telling me stories about my family history since I was a girl. To Helen Brooks, Reana Jenkins, Ruth Jenkins, Beverly Anderson-Corprew, Ivan A. Hampden, Sr., Jean E. Hampden, Shirley Smith, and Gregory Taylor. Many special thanks to Arthur Jenkins and Florence Shaw who both have been my main source of inspiration in writing this book of poems, and including my family history.

Special acknowledgments to Angela Batchelor, whom with her insight, creativity and dedication to ensure the book's completion that this book was done with God's grace.

Dedication

Brown Sugar
You're teaching me
how to love so unconditionally!

Foreword

I had hoped to have the family I have. Regardless of being loved by them or not, I knew they were mine. I have good people in my life today. Growth is still apparent with many of us who are getting older, trying to fulfill our goals and dreams. That is why this book is so important to me, and my family members, who have been telling our story to each other for so long.

My story of love started when I was 15 years old and fell in love with Anthony. He was a young man who loved me, too. It was a love lost and never to be found again, until now.

Unconditional love is common for children who grow up in a safe and loving environment. Yet, when we become adults, we grow so far from what our basic needs really are and try to actively achieve our goals. In the past, a woman's goal was to have children and a family, regardless of having a loving man.

These photos are of my parents and ancestors whose goals of love and family have brought me here to this page. May God bless them and the uniqueness of their loving ways.

Yvonne Hampden

Contents

A Woman's Lover..1
Mystified by His Presence 3
Sunday...5
Untitled 1 7
Friends and Lovers 9
When Only Men Are Noble 11
Caressing Me..13
Why Do They Call It "Playing House?" 15
A Beat Every Hour...17
Don't Try to Understand Me..19
A.M. Morning..21
Miquel 23
Mi Amor 25
My Lover..27
Haiki 1...29
Milk and Cookies 31
Love Is..33
Love Bug 35
Boda...37
I Always Have...39
Love Always…O.K.!..41
Because I Love Him 43
Presence Is a Virtue!...45
Brown Sugar..46
True Womanhood...48
Thomas-Smith-Hampden Family Tree..................................53
Crawford-Smith-Hampden Family Tree.................................54

A Woman's Lover

What is love but the soul's
        Cry to be complete with God?

To make peace after the storm
        Is over, and laugh at the moon
        For all her secrets she reveals.

Who is a man who loves the
        Nurturing hand of a woman?
        To know her,
                        And see the glow
She instills in his eye.

He can no longer tell lies,
        His heart is so full.
        And, she touches him so tenderly
        In his heart,
                He cleanses her soul of
All others.

Who is a man, who is he,
        Who truly loves a woman?

The breath and the exhale come
        Together…
        I'll come and he'll come…

              We'll come as one… .

Left to right: Gladstone Hampden, b. July 7th, 1899 in Barbados, West Indies. d. March 15th, 1995. Employed as a Police Officer NYC, NY. Son of Edgar Vivian Hampden and Florence Juniss. Millicent Mary Seton, b. October 10th, 1899 in Port of Spain, Trinidad, d. July 15, 1961. Millicent Mary's parents were born in Lagos, Nigeria, Ibo Tribe. Paternal Grandparents. They had 10 children. My dad, Ivan A. Hampden, Sr., was their fifth child.

Mystified by His Presence

Mystified by his presence
    In the sense it leaves
        Me feeling whole, waiting for
            The words he says…

That have taken me, and are swaying me
    Straight towards him, and his blues
        Pull me closer, like a thunder-storm,
            My heart sings of rain.

Sunday

Ear full…
            Joy, love, time

Peace of mind

And I am saying it, telling it kindly.

He walked in and changed everything,

His face, my embrace.

Tall and sure. Employed.

Smooth — He said to me "I enjoy you."

…Mind full…

Young and strong. I stared at him,

His youthfulness. I know him now,

Nearly old. His mind sharp

As a bull's eye. Me…so shy

He remembered me… every time

I passed him by.

Untitled 1

He doesn't know how much she
    loves him.
        That when he's not
With her, her soul is an empty hole
Wasting her body away.
        He keeps

Calling to her — bitch this and bitch that.
And although she is sometimes clumsy,
she can't quite understand his bitching.

So, she lays low for his punches
and remembers the before-hand of the
lovemaking.
        Yeah! He speaks
out-loud, mumbling her heart's
   desires.
        He knows of her
love.

        He and she

        The beginning, and a
means to an end... .

Untitled 1

He doesn't know how much she
    loves him.
           That when he's not
With her, her soul is an empty hole
Wasting her body away.
        He keeps
Calling to her — bitch this and bitch that.
And although she is sometimes clumsy,
she can't quite understand his bitching.

So, she lays low for his punches
and remembers the before-hand of the
lovemaking.
          Yeah! He speaks
out-loud, mumbling her heart's
    desires.
          He knows of her
love.

        He and she

        The beginning, and a
means to an end... .

Friends and Lovers...

Lying together in bed
                       No one is the other's friend
Or lover anymore. We move away from each other,
Hating to feel the tenderness of the touch of one
Another. We no longer search or look into each other's
Eyes for the love that has always been there.
                                ...I
Angry at you. You angry at me. No longer sharing
The feelings that come from accepting one another
For who we really are...
                 They say that action speaks
Louder than words, but I am sure that if we spoke
Of words our actions act upon, the warmth and the
Strength we feel within us would pull us back together
As friends
           And
                 Lovers...
                           (...in bed).

Left to right: Benjamin Anderson of Irish and German descent. White gentleman farmer who owned over 750 acres of land in 1850. He donated 137 acres of land to his children. He also donated land for the Anderson Chapel, and for the Anderson Academy school, both in Texas. Priscilla (Katie) Anderson was a Native American Indian (Blackfoot).

Benjamin fell in love with Katie at a cattlemen's convention. It is said that she was a prostitute, and he made a lady out of her. Katie had a daughter before she married Benjamin. Her daughter's name was Amanda. Maternal grandfather's great grandparents.

When Only Men Are Noble

How can I feel like a woman?
By his caress
His gentle tenderness

His naked eye
The way he never says goodbye

The shy way he says, hi!

Why do I feel like a woman?
Because his tender touch
Makes me want so much.

The tears I cry, never wanting to lie.
He, so warm,
               Settling the storm.
Rain is no more, no more water
On the floor. Until I die..,
I will never be the woman I longed to be
Needing so badly his loving arms.

My approach, so fiery,
His suspicions, so leery.

Just wrap your arms around me
Pull me close and astound me
Feeling cuddled and so real
The way I want to feel.

When Only Men Are Noble

Womanly,
           I'll be a lady another day
Please stay...
           The nights here are so long
I'm not strong. I need
           The desires of a loving man
Please take my hand.

Cry in my arms...
           Our destiny lies in the cards
...so unwomanly of me to say,
           May I lay with you?

Will I be worthy of you?
Fighting to be a wife, this life
I get from you, inside of God
           It's so hard
To be a woman...
It's so hard to need the softness of a man.

Caressing Me...

The scent of your body
                arouses
Desires unforeseen in me...

I want to caress you tenderly upon my breast
And hold you there, still,
Until the night is over and dawn
Comes upon us, and reawakens
My every emotion.

Desperately, I wallow in
             and
             out of your arms
Making joyful advances to swallow all of you that
Belongs to me...
             joyfully
Tenderly... .
             Everything is still.
Time has taken our space,
And has made everything still and peaceful.

Your dark color envelopes the night... .
Another day passes us by; another day gone and
We are still making love.

Desperately we hold on to each other's brawn
So to remain free of our quake of loneliness.
At last, this unforeseen desire has replenished itself.

All questions still unanswered remain with us,
And, the love,
             The desire, + the reasoning
All vanish, 'cause baby, now we are one... .

Ivan A. Hampden, Sr. and Jean E. Smith, married May 8th, 1955. My parents.

Why Do They Call It "Playing House?"

The children in bed,
They ate on time
And said their prayers.

My man, home late,
Worked overtime again.
A baby on the way, and
Many bills to pay.

I have to make a plate.
My man, again, home late.
Make beds, tell stories
For my children to believe in.

Sewing holes in old clothes,
And cleaning fingerprints
From walls, cleaning dirty draws
My house may have company soon.

When I rest I make plans,
Family stands,
No setbacks
But, with a woman's loving touch
And a hard-working man
Love goes far, God!, I know
Why we are… .

Why Do They Call It "Playing House?"

Why do they call this playing house?
Nurturing a seed, sown,
And reaped with care.

I call my house real…
Family is a familiar sound
When my child feeds off my breast,
My man has paid the rent.

My man comes home needing
My loving tenderness.
Lord knows how I remember those familiar sounds.

A Beat Every Hour

Please don't make me wait
For your heavens, my opening gate
My mind is in a terrible state
Tell me, is this my fate?

I don't know anymore
My heart so terribly sore
Has my spirit tore?
Forgive me Lord
I just wanted to give that feeling of joy.

Now my heart, so sour
Skipping a beat every hour
Slowly needing a new form of power
I can't shout it any louder
A new beat needed for the hour.

Don't Try to Understand Me, Just Know Who I Am...

That damn rejection
  Reaching over and touching me,
                        Again.

No caring, just sex and
                        Fun

On its mind.

                        Not ever jealous

Just an uncomplicated

                        Non-suspicious

Nature
Of the unlikely kind.
Bred from an unaffectionate

                        Gentle bitchiness

With its lack of compassion
Just downright unfamiliar

Rejection.

                        Damn...!

Edgar Vivian Hampden migrated to Barbados from Nigeria. Edgar worked making kegs on a ship and paid for his freedom. He became a plantation manager in Barbados and married the wealthy plantation owner's daughter Florence Juniss, from England. Her family disowned her. Great grandfather later became employed as a tinsmith, plumber, and Minister in Barbados. They lived in a shack and had seven children. My grandfather, Gladstone Hampden, was their only son.

A.M. Morning...

Because of you
           My days don't
Hurt anymore...

Going to bed with you each night
Helps me feel as sweet as pie.
Waking with you in the morning
Is honey in my tea.

Your love and life are so perfect for me.

The closeness is so comfortable (when
I tell you how I feel, I feel closer to you).
I can't wait to tell you!

I'm hoping you'll call this morning before you
Start work...
I'm looking out of an oval shaped, decorated window.
The sun is rising into the sky,
           It's getting so bright.

That's when I think of you, and begin to wonder
About last night...
           I felt a funny, uncomfortable
Feeling last night while we were loving each other.

A.M. Morning...

...Well, when you come home tonight (this evening, rather) I won't be here.
                    Then, you'll come and get me.
You'll know where I am, and you'll wait 'til I come out to you. Then you'll take me home... .

I can't sleep anymore this morning. I want to!
Not to dream anymore, but to feel and remember you in my comfort.

Miquel

Like the bird and the fish
The air and the sea
Like a mirror is an ocean
The reality and the dream.

As Michael is Miquel
And Mikail's Navy Blue
Is a sailor with a vision
Will make all my dreams come true.

I row my boat down stream
A river of love I offer
'Til night and day are one again,
As we sail into forever.

I once stopped walking on my
Own two feet, and sat inside a car.
You drove, I was a passenger
Together we went far.

Now, in the hands of God
We've found a love so true,
And, with the promise of tomorrow
I give my heart to you.

Miquel

My heart is a shield
To keep away the cold,
To block the wind of a sail,
As a sail will bring us home.

When a sea gull comes near
To eat the bait you buy
You feed him generously full
And far away he flies.

You take out your fishing pole
And you continue to fish
The ocean reflects the sun
Until the tide comes in.

Mi Amor

Mi amor, ben aqui
Mi corazon no esta bien
Yo no tengo vida
Porque no te tengo a ti.

Por favor, ben aqui
Ben a mi casa
Mi casa es tu casa
Tengo mucho amor en mi corazon

Para ti, para mi y mucho mas.

Ben aqui !ahora!
No hay mucho tiempo
Porque yo necesito tu amor y
Tu necesitas mi amor
Ben pronto, por favor…,

Te espero con amor
?mi amor, donde estas?

Interpreted by Mileida Gutierrez

My Lover

Lover… come here
My heart is not good.
I have no life
Because I don't have you.

Please, come here.
Come into my house
My house is your house…
I have much love in my heart
For you, for me, and much more.

Come here, Now!
There isn't much time
Because I need your love, and
You need my love
Hurry, please…

I am waiting with love
Lover… where are you?

Gladstone Hampden at age 25. My paternal grandfather.

Haiki 1

For my 28th birthday
I want to be on a wet sandy beach
On a moonlit night
Making love to a stranger.

Left to right: George W. Anderson, believed to be with his second wife in this photo, her name is unknown. His first wife's name was Margaret. George was one of four sons of Benjamin and Priscilla (Katie) Anderson. George had several children. His daughter Lena Mae Anderson Smith Crawford had expanded the family. Lena had 10 children. One was Marcus Smith,Sr., my maternal grandfather.

Milk & Cookies

Friends are like milk and cookies;
You need two of them to share,
Or you can't really have a party.

Makes no sense, I know,
But only milk and cookies understand
The loneliness of a warmed cold winter's night
Shared by someone...

That's how it was with you... I'll never forget
The sharing.

Milk & Cookies

Friends are like milk and cookies;
You need two of them to share,
Or you can't really have a party.

Makes no sense, I know,
But only milk and cookies understand
The loneliness of a warmed cold winter's night
Shared by someone...

That's how it was with you... I'll never forget
The sharing.

Love is...

Sometimes good,

Sometimes free.

Love gives, never leaves.

I need… to be loved …forever.

Love me forever lover… will you… give… lover... be love to me.

Be my lover… lover… lover come close.

Love Bug

Have you ever loved a junkie?

Fed him, spoon in mouth, prayed

His sperm don't poison your spout,

...and rubbish won't come out...

Love a man / give him a grand stand,

And swallow his pain.

    Be so desperately ashamed

When people came a/round

    vein,

Needle-stained, blood-red, hungry

    For love...

A junkie's turn to rush.

Cold-stone busted, turned trick...

And can't get his dick hard...

I've gone too, too far loving a junkie.

But I loved him... and my loneliness out

That spout sometimes was so full...

Left, right and center: Gladys Thomas Smith b. April 22nd, 1913 in Philidelphia, PA, d. February 16th, 1978. Employed as a civil servant, NYC, NY. Grandmother Gladys' parents were both Blackfoot Native American. Marcus Smith, Sr. b. January 21st, 1913 in Houston, Texas, d. August 16th, 1982. Grandfather was a business owner in Bronx, NY. Maternal grandparents. Ivan A. Hampden, Jr. nicknamed, Peppy. My oldest sibling, and first born to Ivan, Sr. and Jean Hampden.

Boda

Why do people have to die?
As if to reflect the heavens in the sky
I did not really want to cry
I knew somehow it was a lie.

As if to think of you as gone
The rumbling thunder of a storm
The trampling kindness of the wind
Each cold breeze, a sea hawk's fins.

And, as the night turns into day
I know it's true, you've gone away.

I Always Have...

I love him,
> I always have.
>> Before I knew him even so this is true.

Time struggled to bring us together, all our strengths used for that identical purpose.
In our meeting place we secretly understood how time pursued us.
It's useless...
I definitely could not fight it or come to understand the pain of it all.
Damn, this page is long. Is it secretly drawing me closer to you?
I love you!
Only because I did not come to be true to myself before I met you...
I remember thinking how I knew it all, oh! A woman I have not been,
Finally reaching an open end to truths and enclosing on falsehoods
You see, I am honestly in love with you...
Passion/desperation has ended/I'm cool knowing you love me too....
I'm cool knowing you love me too too too,
So I'm not desperate anymore, anymore came so close
To needing you ever so more/ ever so more is such a nice destiny...
See you soon...!

Love Always, O.K.!

We've loved each other always
Stuck side by side by soul
My heart titters, yours may tatter
Feathers fall from pillows.

Love's o.k., always, with you
Right by my side
We've loved each other always
Don't worry, you'll always be mine.

I miss your love, your goodness
I miss my heart, yours and mine
Tell me I'm still silly
Don't forget, to you, I'm still fine.

I miss that titter tatter
Your heart beating close, listen to mine.
We've loved each other always
Love held together by the tide.

Because I Love Him

Why do men try to hurt us to gain control?
They go to bed without you, maybe with someone else.
They use your mind, become unkind, and sometimes
They won't let you touch their warm, gentle bodies.
Or, they won't touch yours... Then you yearn
And crave for your man, and at that instant you
Wonder if he's truly yours and if, maybe, you're
The only one who's sincere in the relationship.

What does a man want from you? Your time?
Your body? Your money?
Your love?
Can't he truly just accept you as you are?
Someone who wants to work, maybe at home
And who wants to bear his children
And grow old with him (together).
You and he together, forever...

Like when you were sixteen and so f/i/n/e,
Everything fit right (tight), and you didn't
Need makeup.
All the guys on the block wanted you
But you were off limits, because you were his
And you couldn't take up with anyone else.

There's nothing like being young and IN LOVE...

The passion is an uprising desire to conquer
Your life in one cum. Then you grow up and
Maybe lose each other. It happened like that with me,
...see...

Because I Love Him

But I've found someone whose passion has
Aroused me and I've felt sixteen again, but I'm
Now losing him. Tell me, dear Lord, what do I do?
I'm praying to you...
       Well, time will tell, but
Tell me this: Is this 'what becomes of love?'
Is this the answer to one of my questions I wrote
In one of my poems? 'What is life? Or is it, life is what it is?'
But yeah, to hell with it. So what you love him...
Why should he want you?

Are you intelligent?
Are you looking for work?
Do you clean your house?
Is his dinner ready when he comes home from a hard day's work?

All these have become valid questions to your femininity
And his masculinity...
He loves you,
       He came home... .

Presence Is a Virtue!

Presence
       is a virtue
            'cause it's
Only when you're near me
       that I breathe
So well.
       My life comes
            to a new
Height, thinking clearly
            of you.
                I dread
                      your absence,

Loneliness (sunders) me
      aimlessly,
I look at your picture and dream daydreams
(I know you so very well…)
Reckless desires that go nowhere

Waiting for you…

Brown Sugar

You are teaching me how
To love, again, so unconditionally!

Brown Sugar, I'm cold as ice
But you, Brown Sugar,
Take all of the pain away;
All the hurt away…

I'm healing with you,
Opening my mind and heart again.
You remind me of my first love,
So totally unconditional.

Brown Sugar, you are so fine,
Sweet as molasses, a touch
Of honey in my tea
You are everything to me!

I care so much about you,
In my own funny kind of way.
My heart flutters,
I keep dreaming of you.

Brown Sugar, your voice so tender
When you speak to me,
Eyes warming my heart
Touching my soul.

Brown Sugar

The passion I feel is so real
In my heart for you.
My heart, and my virginity
Are so totally connected.

When I think of loving
Someone and being loved
I think and dream of you,
I feel so connected to you.

Brown Sugar, sometimes I feel
You are in my heart, connected
To my soul,

You are kind, you are sweet,
I'm so glad you found me,
Brown Sugar.

True Womanhood

Author's note: "True Womanhood" *is a family memoir, which my Aunt Shirley of Merced, California, gave to me in 2005. I kept the letter without thoughts of publishing it in my book. However, after Aunt Shirley read* "True Womanhood" *she said* "It is right for this book." *The date and the author of* "True Womanhood" *is unknown. Aunt Shirley believes the letter was written in the early 1900's, and we do know the letter was written for Mr. Chairman and members of the Sunday School Convention of the Houston District.*

Mr. Chairman and members of the Sunday School Convention of the Houston District:

Womanhood is that principal action which characterizes the Women of any race. Of this, there may be mentioned two distinct classes of Womanhood. Namely false-womanhood, and true-womanhood.

False-womanhood is that element in women which makes them unfit for the responsibilities of womanly duties. True-womanhood is evidenced by all of the personal charms and accomplishments which make a woman the highest product of our Christian civilization. True-womanhood is that, that is to be most desired by us both as men and women of our race. Because our writer has said that no race can rise above its women, therefore if we wish to rise high in the affairs of the world and to take our place along side the other races of the earth we must elevate the character of our women.

The question comes to us now, how can we encourage true-womanhood? What can we do to bring the young women of our race to realize the value of true-womanhood? The answer is, we must first put a premium on true-womanhood and stamp of disapproval on false-womanhood.

The girls of the race must be taught the value of virtue and honesty. They must learn to be true to themselves and then they will be true to others.

Virtue and honesty do not consist in a beautiful face, nor in fine showy

True Womanhood

clothes, but is that rich gem within any woman which makes her think more of those things which elevate and uplift, than any of the worldly things about us.

One thing that has done more to discourage true-womanhood has been the fact that the men of our race have put more value on the women of questionable character than they have on the pious Christian women.

If a woman is pretty and dresses well and is popular, our men flock around her to honor her, without considering her moral worth. The professional society woman of this day and time, and the women who always seeking prominence among men are doing much to destroy the true-womanhood of the race. They are dragging the emblem of true-womanhood in the dirt of slander and gossips. They are attaching the reputation of false-womanhood to the glory and honor of true-womanhood, for they, like fools, rush in where angels fear to tread. This class of women must be denounced and put aside.

We must give more attention to that class of our young women who are not blessed with beauty nor riches, and encourage them to stand up for their principals of true-womanhood.

We must teach them to know that if they are not pretty and popular, if they cannot dress in elegant style they can nevertheless be true women and be rewarded for their worth.

We have thousands of honest poor girls who are not noticed. We must go to these and with the influence of education and Christianity mold them into garlands of gold.

We owe it to the race, we owe it to ourselves and we owe it to this great church of Allen, to go on record as encouraging true-womanhood and virtue in all walks of life.

Pages one and two of the original letter, "True Womanhood," written more than one hundred years ago, is yellowed, tattered and taped but still resonates a powerful message for the Smith-Hampden family.

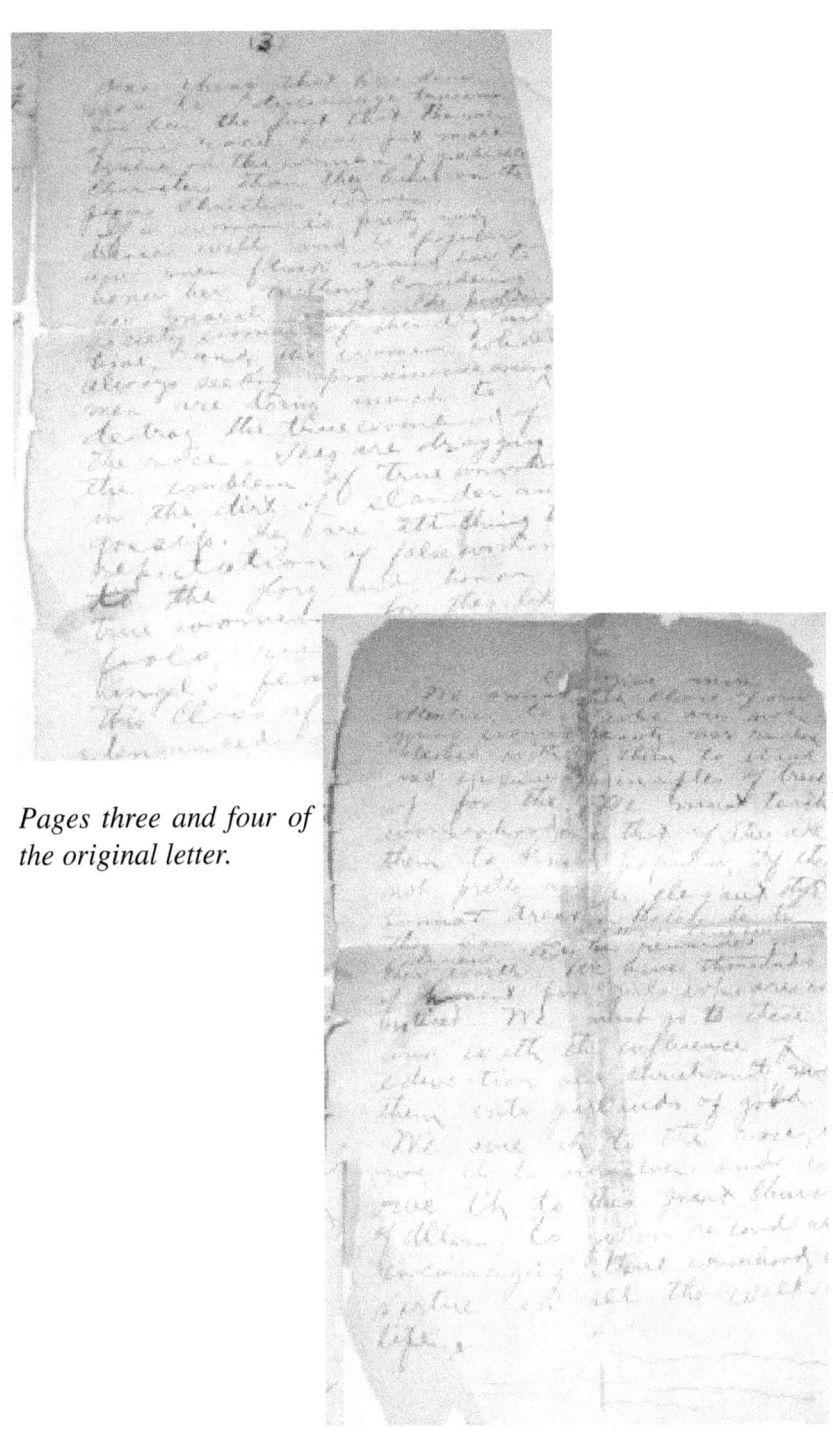

Pages three and four of the original letter.

The original letter, "True Womanhood" written more than one hundred years ago, is a family memoir to the Smith-Hampden family.

Thomas-Smith-Hampden Family

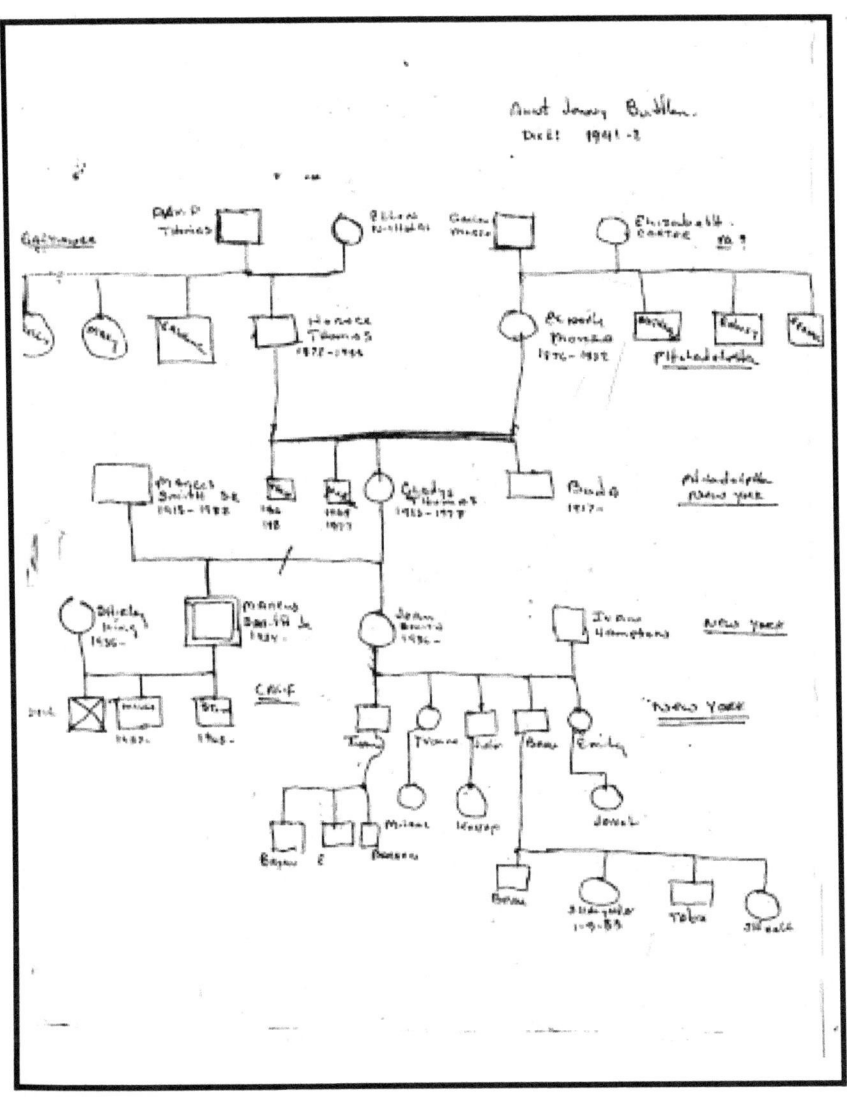

CRAWFORD-SMITH-HAMPDEN FAMILY

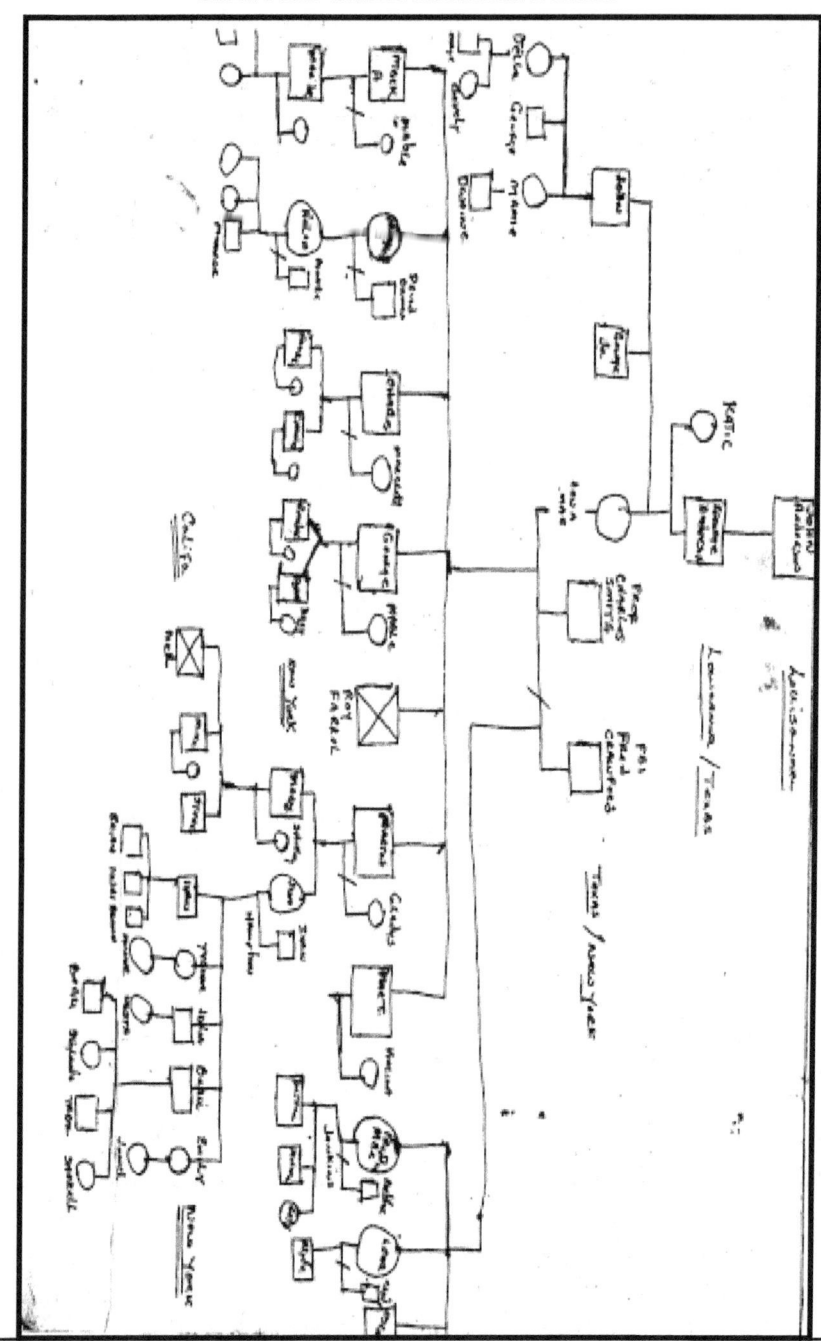

Shake up the World!

Just a little for myself...

The grass is always greener on the other side.

A resurgence of my name.

Free my ancestors from their pain. For everything they have given to me, find the truth about my family tree; my family history. Free my ancestors from their early grave that has caused me so much pain, in the aftermath of change.

Late cousin Melvin Jenkins on the Blackjack III, Yacht, on the waters near New Rochelle, NY.

A Woman's Lover, written as a family memoir, is coupled with historic photos, captions, and poems to touch a reader's heart. *A Woman's Lover* is a soul healing account of years of family history that will have you searching for the love stories in your genealogy. This is Yvonne Hampden's second book of poetry. She lives in Yonkers, New York.

www.ingramcontent.com/pod-product-compliance
Lightning Source LLC
Chambersburg PA
CBHW071841290426
44109CB00017B/1897